Facilitator's Guide

D0473613

DIFFERENTIATING
the High School
Classroom

Solution Strategies for 18 Common Obstacles

KATHIE F. NUNLEY

CORWIN PRESS
A SAGE Company
Thousand Oaks, CA 91320

For information:

Corwin Press
A SAGE Company
2455 Teller Road
Thousand Oaks, California 91320
www.corwinpress.com

SAGE Ltd.
1 Oliver's Yard
55 City Road
London EC1Y 1SP
United Kingdom

SAGE India Pvt. Ltd.
B 1/I 1 Mohan Cooperative
    Industrial Area
Mathura Road, New Delhi 110 044
India

SAGE Asia-Pacific Pte. Ltd.
33 Pekin Street #02-01
Far East Square
Singapore 048763

Printed in the United States of America

ISBN: 978-1-4129-6595-8

This book is printed on acid-free paper.

08   09   10   11   12   10   9   8   7   6   5   4   3   2   1

Acquisitions Editor:	Carol Chambers Collins
Editorial Assistant:	Brett Ory
Production Editor:	Melanie Birdsall
Copy Editor:	Bill Bowers
Typesetter:	C&M Digitals (P) Ltd.
Proofreader:	Cheryl Rivard
Cover Designer:	Karine Hovsepian

Contents

About the Author

Kathie F. Nunley, EdD, delights teachers from around the world with her practical solutions to the challenges of teaching in today's diverse classrooms. A noted speaker at state, national, and international conferences, Dr. Nunley is the author of many books and articles on brain biology and teaching in mixed-ability classrooms. Her work has been used by institutions and publications around the globe, including *Family Circle* magazine, *Canada Living,* and *The Washington Post.* She is the developer of the Layered Curriculum method of instruction and has worked more than 15 years as a classroom teacher in both urban and suburban schools. A mother of four, she continues her research, writing, and educational consulting from her 1800s farmhouse in New England.

Introduction

This facilitator's guide is designed to accompany the study of the book *Differentiating the High School Classroom: Solution Strategies for 18 Common Obstacles* by Kathie F. Nunley. It offers a framework for guiding group facilitators involved in professional development workshops. It summarizes each of Nunley's 18 most common obstacles of secondary differentiation and includes discussion starters, workshop activities, and application ideas as well as handouts and worksheets for use as support material. Reading this guide will give facilitators a solid background for successfully leading a study of the book.

For **independent study**, participants may wish to:

1. Read the assigned chapter in the book.
2. Reflect on (or answer) the discussion questions.
3. Complete the "Putting It Into Practice" assignments.

For **small, one-day workshops,** facilitators can guide the participants to:

1. Read the entire book in advance.
2. Participate in the discussion questions.
3. Take part in one or more of the activities.
4. Complete many of the "Extended Activities" on their own after the workshop.

For **workshops that run over an extended period of time,** facilitators may wish to:

1. Assign prereading of specific chapters in the book.
2. Participate in the discussion questions.
3. Have participants complete one or more of the "Putting It Into Practice" extended activities and come prepared to report their experiences at the next class.

Additional Resources for Facilitators

Corwin Press also offers a free 16-page resource titled *Tips for Facilitators,* which includes practical strategies and tips for guiding a successful meeting. The information in this section describes different professional development opportunities, the principles of effective professional development, some characteristics of an effective facilitator, the responsibilities of the facilitator, and practical tips and strategies to make the meeting more successful. *Tips for Facilitators* is available for free download at the Corwin Press Web site (www.corwinpress.com, under "Resources/Tips for Facilitators").

We recommend that facilitators download a copy of *Tips for Facilitators* and review the characteristics and responsibilities of facilitators and professional development strategies for different types of work groups and settings.

Chapter-by-Chapter Study Guide

Differentiating the High School Classroom: Solution Strategies for 18 Common Obstacles

by Kathie F. Nunley

Welcome and Workshop Starter

Time: 10–20 minutes (depending on group size)
Materials: Overhead 1: Workshop Starter and the textbook *Differentiating the High School Classroom: Solution Strategies for 18 Common Obstacles*

Begin by introducing yourself and welcoming your participants. After an overview of the schedule and meeting times, introduce the course with the overhead of the book's dedication (from page xii in the text; also see Overhead 1: Workshop Starter at the end of this guide).

Allow participants to introduce themselves and share one or two of the "unique gifts" they possess and bring to the group.

Introduction: I Just Can't Do That in MY School/Classroom/Situation

Chapter Summary

This chapter emphasizes that while problems are inherent to life, success and satisfaction come from viewing these as opportunities for creativity. Rather than focusing a great deal of energy on describing problems, let's focus on solutions.

The author shares some of her background as an example of how one can use life's challenges as a growth opportunity.

The chapter concludes with a brief introduction of the two primary factors that have highlighted the need in recent years for differentiation at the high school level:

1. Neuropsychological research has confirmed the great variation that exists among developing brains.
2. Changes in America's classrooms have created much more diversity than ever before. Teachers must reexamine traditional strategies in light of these changes.

Discussion Questions

1. Discuss the relationship between problem solving and creativity.
2. Elaborate on the author's statement, "Struggles build character and intelligence."
3. What research or professional development presentations have you been exposed to that shed light on the need for differentiation?
4. What knowledge of differentiation do you bring with you today?

Activity

● *Brainstorming "Problems"*

Time: 15 minutes
Materials: Chart paper or overhead projector and write-on transparencies

The purpose of this activity is to learn to separate problems into two categories: those you have the power to change and those you currently do not. Then focus your energy on those situations in which you can take action to make a difference.

In a large group, with a scribe or two, brainstorm all the obstacles to differentiation teachers currently feel they have in their classrooms. Put a time limit—say, 10 or 15 minutes—on the brainstorming session. Have the scribe write these obstacles on large chart paper, or the facilitator can write them on an overhead. Go back over the list, and circle or otherwise highlight issues that group members feel they do have some power to change. (*Note to facilitator:* You may want a brief discussion here of how, for the rest of this workshop, we will simply set aside those issues that we currently cannot change, so that we can focus our energy on those things we can change.)

Putting It Into Practice

(*Extended activity based on* Brainstorming "Problems")

Time: 15 minutes
In small groups of three or four, have participants share some ideas for how they could take action immediately to effect some change on some of the problems listed. Given time constraints, they may want to discuss which ones they value the most and discuss a commitment to take some action.

Journal Prompt

Write about a personal challenge you have faced, outside of education, that you feel became an opportunity for creativity and satisfying solutions.

Chapter 1 Obstacle: I Long to Return to the Good Old Days

Chapter Summary

This chapter starts with a personal story to illustrate an important problem with high school teaching—diffusion of responsibility and "lost" students. Our large institutions make it easy for students to slip through the cracks, unnoticed by their many teachers despite our best intentions.

A description of the issue includes the unspoken hope of many teachers that the huge variation we see among our students and this heavy push for differentiation will just go away. Many of us have a mental model of school in bygone days, when students were all successful in a traditional format. Many current authors of education books also make mention of a need to "return to the good old days."

The author includes a brief history of the concept of high school in America, starting in the late 1700s and moving through our high schools today. What is of important note is the huge change in the percentage of the population that attends high school. As recently as midway through the last century, most Americans did not graduate from high school.

It's also important to note that since the beginning, high schools have struggled with a single purpose. They have always been torn between educating students for the sake of education, preparing them for college, or preparing them for the business community.

This chapter also includes the reasoning for the additional levels of junior high and junior college. These were added in an attempt to fix any problems that may have been missed so that all students entered the next educational level functioning with the same skills.

Discussion Questions

1. What mental model do you have about high school? What did your high school look like in terms of students attending and the teaching methodology used?
2. What was the cultural makeup of your high school when you attended? If you did not have students with moderate and severe learning disabilities included in your classroom, where were those students during the school day?
3. Look at the chart in Figure 1.1 in the text, *Differentiating the High School Classroom: Solution Strategies for 18 Common Obstacles* (page 8). What does this mean for high school teachers? What changes should teacher preparation programs have made during the last half century?

Activity

● *Research Primary Sources for Historical Perspective*

(Extended activity)

Research the increasing diversity in your workplace using your campus library, microfiche at your local newspaper, archived yearbooks, and so on. View primary sources as far back as you can (preferably from when your high school was built). Look at enrollment, graduation rates, class sizes, ethnic diversity, and special education arrangements. Be prepared to report back to the group and share what you find.

Journal Prompt

If you are one who has longed for the "good old days," what did they look like? What are the realities of that model in terms of students who do not fit the traditional mold?

Chapter 2 Obstacle: I Thought I *Was* Differentiating

Chapter Summary

This chapter deals with some of the misconceptions of differentiation. Just including a variety of teaching strategies during the week does not necessarily mean you are differentiating instruction. True differentiation means you are offering a variety of strategies for each learning objective. (*Note to facilitator:* You may want to use the overhead here in your discussion. See Overhead 2: Differentiated Instruction at the end of this guide.)

Differentiation also means that you differentiate not just the learning activities (the process) but also the assessment and content as well.

Teachers may be uncomfortable with having multiple activities occurring at the same time in the classroom. It's important for teachers to remember to start slowly, with just two or three activity choices, so that both teacher and student can ease into the new system.

Discussion Questions

1. Although using a variety of teaching strategies is essential to a differentiated classroom, simply using them is not necessarily differentiating instruction. Why?
2. Of the three areas to differentiate (content, process, and product), which do you find the most challenging and why?
3. What are some of your fears of allowing students choice?
4. On page 14, Practical Solution Idea 2.1 discusses "running assignments." What are some running assignments that may fit your teaching area?
5. On page 15, Practical Solution Idea 2.2 discusses using interdisciplinary assignments as a way to differentiate content. What are some interdisciplinary assignments that may fit your teaching area?

Activity

● *Differentiating All Three Learning Areas*

Time: 20–40 minutes
Materials: Copy of Activity Sheet 1: Differentiating All Three Learning Areas for each participant; and the textbook *Differentiating the High School Classroom: Solution Strategies for 18 Common Obstacles*

The text mentions three learning areas that need to be differentiated: content, process, and product. Choose a unit topic from your current content area. With a colleague, generate some ideas for differentiating each of these three areas. (See Activity Sheet 1: Differentiating All Three Learning Areas at the end of this guide.)

Putting It Into Practice

(Extended activity)

Referring to page 15 in the book, design a lesson plan for your classroom in the coming week in which you offer students some choice about how they learn a specific objective. Not all learning objectives need to have choice, but try to have several.

Chapter 3 Obstacle: I Teach the Way I Was Taught

Chapter Summary

This chapter begins with a description of the problem, which is that we teach as we were taught because:

1. It may be all we know.
2. It apparently worked for us, so it must work for anyone.

The problem with this fundamental judgment error (I learned this way, so you should too) is that this type of thinking excludes the majority of our students. The traditional textbook-lecture methodology is very rigid and focuses on a small range of students. Given the huge increase in diversity in our schools, coupled with unprecedented political pressure, we must offer a variety of instructional strategies if we want to include the majority of our students in the learning process.

In order to learn other ways to teach, we must expose ourselves to other models. We need to look outside our immediate work area into other educational arenas, such as elementary schools, adult education, community schools, business and technical trade schools, and alternative education settings.

The chapter concludes with practical solution strategies teachers can use to become more familiar with alternative ways of teaching.

Discussion Questions

1. Reflect on your high school days. What types of teaching strategies were used? Which did you find held your attention?

2. Think of the last lesson you taught in your classroom. How would you have taught it if you had no books, no pencils, and no paper and you had to limit your lecture to only half the class period?

3. If you have children, nieces, or nephews, discuss how each of them is different in the types of classrooms and assignments they respond best to.

4. When you attended high school or college, were you ever surprised to find you enjoyed a class? What do you think caused the surprise?

Activities

● *Search for and Discuss Alternative Teaching Approaches*

Time: 20–30 minutes

Materials: Internet access and the textbook *Differentiating the High School Classroom: Solution Strategies for 18 Common Obstacles*

With a partner, do an online search for alternative ed schools, technical trade schools, and community education programs. Click through the Web pages, looking at the photos they display of their students in a "learning environment." What is going on during these instructional times? Pay attention to the ratio of teacher-led versus student-paced activities. These institutions use photos that would look attractive to prospective students. Lead a discussion about how these scenes may look similar or different from your high school classrooms and why.

● *Brainstorm Outside the Box*

Time: 20–30 minutes

Materials: Pen, paper, and the textbook *Differentiating the High School Classroom: Solution Strategies for 18 Common Obstacles*

Complete Practical Solution Idea 3.3 on page 21 in the book, using one, two, or three of your teaching objectives in an upcoming unit of instruction in your classroom.

Putting It Into Practice

(Extended activity based on Brainstorm Outside the Box*)*

Actually implement some of our ideas in your classroom this week, and come back to share with the group.

Chapter 4 Obstacle: I Don't Know How

Chapter Summary

This chapter describes the development and components of Layered Curriculum, a differentiated teaching model designed specifically for high school. The model is based on adding three components to a traditional high school classroom:

1. *Choice:* Offering students a variety of assignment choices from which to learn each teaching objective.
2. *Accountability:* Requiring students to prove they have learned from every assignment. Grade points are awarded for only the actual learning of the objective, rather than the assignments completed.
3. *Encouraging higher-level thinking:* By requiring students to participate and use more and more complex assignments in order to improve their unit grades. Basic knowledge assignments are worth no more than the grade of C, application and manipulation types of assignments can bring the grade up to a B, and critical evaluation assignments can bring the earned grade up to an A.

There are numerous teacher-made examples of Layered Curriculum units available at the Web site Help4Teachers.com.

The facilitator may want to provide copies of some of these sample units from the Help4Teachers.com Web site and/or allow time on the Internet, if available, for teachers to look at additional sample units.

Discussion Questions

1. Read the description of the two fictional students, Walter and Berna, on pages 25–26. Discuss specific examples of how you have seen similar situations in your own school or classroom.
2. Have we evolved a system of education that puts so much emphasis on the process of learning (the quality of the poster, project, length, and so on) that we have lost sight of the "product" (has the objective been learned)? Where did students get the idea that they should get credit for simply doing an assignment?
3. What are the merits or problems with linking a grading system to Bloom's Taxonomy? Are there benefits of switching from issuing grades based on "percent correct" to "complexity of thinking"?

Activity

● *Outline a Unit of Layered Curriculum**

Time: 20 minutes
Materials: Copy of Activity Sheet 2: Layered Curriculum for each participant and the textbook *Differentiating the High School Classroom: Solution Strategies for 18 Common Obstacles*. (Optional resource: Layered Curriculum text by Kathie F. Nunley, available through Brains.org)

Either individually or with a partner, outline a unit of Layered Curriculum for an upcoming instructional unit in your classroom. List the main C Layer, B Layer, and A Layer objectives and/or assignment choices. Use the Practical Solution Idea sections on pages 29–30 for help.

Putting It Into Practice

(Extended activity)

Finish and implement the unit of Layered Curriculum in your classroom. Be prepared to report to the group on how things went and get feedback for modifications.

Chapter 5 Obstacle: I Have Too Much Content to Cover

Chapter Summary

When you have a lot of content to teach, the easiest way to cover it all is simply to lecture. In content-heavy courses, this has led to a huge emphasis on teacher lecture. But just hearing material doesn't mean a student "knows" the material. Time must be given to process and assimilate that material.

This chapter includes some of the research supporting the importance of shifting emphasis away from simply filling students' heads with knowledge and toward teaching students the actual process of learning. Given the fast pace of today's world, much of the information and materials our students will deal with in their adult lives are things we are not yet even aware of.

Teachers need to focus on the "big picture" in their discipline rather than on the specific, detailed components. This allows students to be able to apply a basic understanding of the subject to a changing world.

*Layered Curriculum is a trademark developed by and registered to Kathie F. Nunley. More information is available at Help4Teachers.com.

Another reason teachers need to move away from an exclusive lecture format is the physical changes to the attention-focusing regions of the brain brought on by an increase in visual electronic input. The attention spans of today's students are much shorter than they were just a decade or two ago. Research supports the use of more student-centered models, with their perception of self-made choice to increase concentration and ensure that students are attending to the task at hand.

Discussion Questions

1. Why do you think the author included Aesop's Fable "The North Wind and the Sun" to introduce this chapter?
2. Discuss the statement on page 37: "We aren't preparing students for today but for tomorrow."
3. Ask those teachers who have been teaching for more than a few years to share with the group their personal experiences with seeing a shortening of attention spans.
4. What technologies are you currently using in your classroom on a regular basis that had not even been invented when you were in high school?
5. Discuss the Edward Deci quote on page 40.

Activity

● *Poster Session*

Time: 30–45 minutes
Materials: Large chart paper, colored markers, and the textbook *Differentiating the High School Classroom: Solution Strategies for 18 Common Obstacles*

In pairs, create a poster on one of these topics:

- Why Choice?
- May I Have Your Attention, Please?
- Teaching for the Future

Have your group design a poster for your topic. Then present them in a poster session.

Directions for Poster Session

Attach a poster to the wall. Have one team member stay at the poster. The other joins the "tour group." The tour group divides up, and each member goes to see one of the posters, listen to the artist explain it, and ask questions. After one or two minutes, a timer (the facilitator) announces that it's time to move to the next poster. After completing the whole circle, each teammate switches places with his or her partner, and you repeat the presentations for the next tour group.

Putting It Into Practice

(Extended activity)

Implement choice in your classroom this week by completing one of the three Practical Solution Ideas listed on pages 39–40. Report back to the group next week.

Chapter 6 Obstacle: I'm Good at Lecturing

Chapter Summary

Using lecture as the mainstay of teaching is very popular among high school teachers. It remains popular because most teachers are quite comfortable with it and feel they are good at lecturing.

Unfortunately, this has led to an increased push to segregate classrooms, with traditionally gifted students separated from those with alternative learning methods. It has created support for grouping students by ability, when in fact research does not support ability grouping.

Using a lecture-heavy format in a mixed-ability classroom can be a challenge. It frequently leads to a real power struggle between teacher and student.

One of the solution strategies offered in this chapter is that of offering lecture as an option, with additional ways of dealing with the lecture such as "Structured Doodling" or alternative lesson choices.

This chapter includes a discussion on perception versus reality. Sometimes a teacher can take a situation and change a student's emotional response and cooperation simply by changing the perception without altering the reality.

Discussion Questions

1. Discuss the statement on page 41, "Some teachers in fact use this lecture-heavy format as a way to maintain a segregated classroom. By offering only this one teaching strategy, you easily assure yourself a schoolwide reputation that encourages only those traditionally successful students to enroll."
2. Describe your personal experience with lecture. Do you struggle to maintain student attention? Is it a source of classroom management challenges? How have you solved some of these problems?
3. If you wanted to offer your lecture as an optional assignment, what are some other ways students could learn the same basic

information? What concerns do you have about offering lecture as an option rather than a required assignment?

4. Most school rules have "consequences" associated with them. Why are the consequences always for *not* following the rules? Where are the consequences for following the rules?

Activity

- *Rewriting School Rules*

Time: 30 minutes

Materials: Pens, paper, and the textbook *Differentiating the High School Classroom: Solution Strategies for 18 Common Obstacles*

In either a large or small group, write five or six of your school or classroom rules. Reread the section on switching perception on pages 46–48. Can you rewrite your school rules to change the way students perceive the statement?

Journal Prompt

What are some ways you could offer a few options to your students regarding the lecture time in your classroom?

Chapter 7 Obstacle: I Can't See How I Would Grade All Those Different Assignments

Chapter Summary

This chapter discusses both the logistics of grading and keeping a grade register in a differentiated classroom, as well as the philosophical issues of awarding grades.

Several examples of how to set up a grade book are given, including entering scores by unit, by subunit, by objective, or by day. Teachers are encouraged to find which is the easiest for their needs, yet also meets the requirements of their school or district.

The other issue of grading—the philosophical and subjective task of assigning grades—is an area that needs more discussion among educators. Most educators have simply inherited the traditional "percentage of right answers" scale that's been handed down for decades. An undisclosed number of assignments are given, each of which is weighted subjectively by the teacher, and a student's grade is based on the percentage of correct responses given on the assignment.

The subjectiveness and non-uniformity of this system have created a mountain of problems for teachers, students, parents, and communities. Teachers need to spend some time considering how grades are awarded and what the various grades actually mean, and make sure that students are very clear on how these are determined. Of particular note is the meaning of an "F" grade.

Discussion Questions

1. Having looked at the grade book examples on pages 52–54, which one seems to be the best match for your classroom? Are there modifications you may need to make?
2. After reading the quote on page 55 from Henry Morrison's 1926 book on grade scales, discuss in the group what might be a better way to make grading more uniform and less subjective.
3. In your school, is there any distinction between students who fail because they've turned in nothing at all and students who've worked fairly hard but were not able to come up with enough points to earn a passing grade? Should there be a distinction? If so, how would that work?

Activity

● *Design the "Perfect World" Grading Scheme*

Time: 30–45 minutes
Materials: Pens, paper, and the textbook *Differentiating the High School Classroom: Solution Strategies for 18 Common Obstacles*

In groups of three, have a philosophical discussion on what determines whether a child was successful in a class and should earn "credit" for the course. If you were starting with a blank slate, what criteria would you use to validate success in a course? After designing this "perfect world" criterion, share your thoughts with the large group.

Putting It Into Practice

(Extended activity)

In your classroom this week, try one of the "Practical Solution Ideas" listed on page 58 in the book.

Chapter 8 Obstacle: I Thought Differentiated Instruction Was for Elementary Schools

Chapter Summary

One of the biggest differences between elementary teachers and secondary teachers is the depths to which we know our students. The concept of "diffusion of responsibility" allows us to feel okay about the limited knowledge we may have regarding our students.

Our student load is high, and time is limited. It is difficult to know each individual's strengths and weaknesses, so we feel at a disadvantage in designing activities specific to a child.

High school teachers, too, see differentiated instruction as a model that heavily involves learning centers, and our mental model associates those with an elementary classroom.

We don't need to be intimidated by either of these issues. You don't have to tailor assignments for each individual student, and many subjects lend themselves well to having learning centers or resource centers in the room. It's fairly easy to take ideas used in elementary classrooms and adapt them for our more sophisticated subjects and more complex thinking students.

Discussion Questions

1. Why do you think elementary teachers have been a bit faster to jump on the differentiation "bandwagon"?
2. Could you set up two or three resource or information centers in your classroom? How could they be used?
3. In what ways can you supplement your text with reading material at a variety of levels?

Activity

● *Study of "Diffusion of Responsibility"*

Materials: Several articles and Web site definitions for diffusion of responsibility (any general psychology book will contain a brief account of the Kitty Genovese story) and the textbook *Differentiating the High School Classroom: Solution Strategies for 18 Common Obstacles*

The facilitator reads the Kitty Genovese story to the group (easily found in nearly every psychology text or on the Internet). Have members of the group read various definitions, articles, and descriptions of diffusion of responsibility.

Discuss some solution strategies for overcoming this phenomenon as high school teachers. Reread the story of "Luke" in *Differentiating the High School Classroom*, pages 1–3. What solution strategies can we implement in our schools to prevent "lost" children?

Putting It Into Practice

(Extended activity)

Reread the Practical Solution Idea 8.4 on page 64. In your classroom this week, offer some assignment options that "teach through art." Be prepared to report back to the whole group.

Chapter 9 Obstacle: I Subscribe to Ability Grouping

Chapter Summary

No one needs to tell a teacher that students are all different and unique. Teachers, in fact, are experts in the extent of children's variation. The mystery lies in why for decades we've held fast to the belief that they can all learn in the same fashion!

Actually, most teachers prefer to have students separated and then segregated in classrooms based on their learning ability, aptitude, or learning style. While teachers may believe this is what is best for the students, the reality is that it is best only (or at least easiest) for the teacher. Students, in fact, learn best in mixed-ability classrooms—and the research is quite robust on this topic.

The adult world is not segregated by ability and aptitude. We all have to live, work, and play with a variety of people. The current growth in the global marketplace ensures that this variation will at least continue, if not increase. So it is important for students to learn and interact with a variety of learners in school.

When you mix abilities, though, you need to be prepared for the fact that some students will work harder on some tasks than others, and some students will have to work longer than others to master the same concept.

Discussion Questions

1. Why do schools and districts adopt only *one* textbook for a subject when they know of the great variety of students they have in the system?
2. Discuss the notion of "giftedness." Perhaps it should be replaced with the term "gifted traditional learner." Can you share some stories of children with significant learning disabilities whom you found to be very gifted in some nontraditional ways?
3. Can you list some special education modifications you've seen allocated to specific children, but that could perhaps benefit a great many students if offered to the whole class as well?
4. Discuss the Rosenthal study in the box on pages 71–72. You may want to find and read the original study. Discuss this in the context of your school.

Activity

● *Offering Whole-Class Modifications*

Time: 20–40 minutes
Materials: The textbook *Differentiating the High School Classroom: Solution Strategies for 18 Common Obstacles* and a list of special education

"accommodations" (as many as you can find, preferably 15–20). (*Note to facilitator:* You will need to make up this list ahead of time. Get ideas from a learning specialist, special educator, or special education Web site. You are looking for things such as note-taker, books-on-tape, extended time, oral testing, oral instructions, and so on.)

In small groups, discuss ways that you could offer some of these accommodations as whole-class accommodations. Are there some ideas here that would benefit many of the students you have in your room? How could these be offered as assignment choices?
Share your work with the whole group.

Putting It Into Practice

(Extended activity)

Implement some of the ideas generated in the task above in your classroom this week. Be prepared to share back with the group.

Chapter 10 Obstacle: I Have Real Logistic Issues

Chapter Summary

Despite a genuine enthusiasm for differentiated instruction, many teachers are hesitant to begin, as they are not sure how to overcome some legitimate restraints, such as liability issues, room size, scheduling concerns, and management of materials.
The solutions here are to set limits and parameters as needed. Some assignments and tasks must be limited to certain areas on certain days.

Discussion Questions

1. What logistics are you facing that are currently preventing you from differentiating? Get feedback from the group about possible solutions.
2. Are there any buddy system opportunities that may work in your building? Can you trade off monitoring students in places such as the library, computer room, or lab?
3. How can you set up material centers in your specific classroom to help students and activities stay organized?

Activity

● *Redesigning Your Classroom*

Time: 30+ minutes
Materials: Plain paper, graph paper, pencils, rulers, and the textbook *Differentiating the High School Classroom: Solution Strategies for 18 Common Obstacles*

Sketch out your current classroom setup. Include the placement of desks, tables, teacher's desk, and so on. Hand your sketch to a colleague and ask them to redesign your classroom to reflect a more student-centered strategy. Working with them, modify the design so that it is something you are comfortable with. Identify resource centers, visually quiet areas of the room, and quiet reading areas. (Consider using an electronic sound screen to create a quiet area.)

Journal Prompt

What ideas have you come up with today to overcome some of the logistic issues that are preventing you from differentiating as much as you'd like?

Chapter 11 Obstacle: I Want My Classroom Under Control

Chapter Summary

The need for control is a strong human requirement. Classroom management problems are frequently just control problems caused when an overzealous teacher's attempts for control run into a student's own need for control.

Much research has been done in this area, and it is important for teachers to understand that all the research continues to show us that, actually, the more we try to control students' behavior, the more they will exhibit poor behavior.

Students fight for control as much as teachers do. A happy compromise leads to a more tranquil classroom and one more conducive to learning.

Discussion Questions

1. Discuss the statement on page 81, "The more we control others, the more their behavior needs to be controlled." (*Note to facilitator:* You may want to actually pull Deci's 1995 study or any of his other research on this issue of control for further study and discussion.)
2. Reread the material on leadership styles on pages 83–84. Discuss the findings of how students behave in autocratic classrooms, laissez-faire classrooms, and democratic classrooms. Discuss each hypothetical classroom also in terms of how students' behavior would or would not change if the teacher stepped out of the room.

Activity

● *Leaders, Coaches, and Conductors*

Time: 25–60 minutes (or extended activity)
Materials: Internet access and the textbook *Differentiating the High School Classroom: Solution Strategies for 18 Common Obstacles*

Have each participant research a great leader, athletic coach, or musical conductor. Find out what qualities he or she possessed that led people to perceive them as great. Bring your report back to the group and draw comparisons to how teachers can exhibit these same qualities in their work with students.

Putting It Into Practice

(Extended activity)

Implement some of the ideas generated in the task above in your classroom this week. Be prepared to share back with the group.

Chapter 12 Obstacle: I Don't Know How to Measure My Students' Learning Styles

Chapter Summary

In the beginning years of differentiated instruction, teachers were told to try to individually match a child's learning "style" with tailored activities. We were under the mistaken impression that students had one preferred style for learning. Much time was spent trying to measure that style so we could offer the appropriate lessons.

However, what the research bore out is that first, it's doubtful that a student's true learning style can be measured with a subjective, paper-and-pencil test. And more important, people's styles change based on subject, perceived difficulty, and self-efficacy in the area. In other words, you may have one style for math, one for English, and yet another for social studies. And your style for math may vary based on how difficult the task is for you.

So measuring a student's learning style is not a requirement (or perhaps not even a possibility) for running a differentiated classroom.

When you require students to learn from an assignment, they will quickly discover their learning style for the task. Simply offer a variety of tasks, require learning to be demonstrated before credit is issued, and you will not need to worry about measuring learning style.

Discussion Questions

1. How does your personal preferred learning style vary by task?
2. Discuss the author's statement on page 90, "Goslin puts in writing what most of us already secretly know: for a small, select group of students, the American education system works exceptionally well. What most of us don't want to talk about or address is the other group, the large group that isn't being served by the system."
3. Do students in your classroom understand the strong relationship between "doing" an assignment and learning from it?

Activity

● *Teach One Objective Through Multiple Learning Styles*

Time: 15 minutes
Materials: The textbook *Differentiating the High School Classroom: Solution Strategies for 18 Common Obstacles* and a list of teaching objectives from a variety of subjects (e.g., *students will understand the symbiotic relationships of commensalism, parasitism, and mutualism; students will be able to multiply a fraction by an integer; students will be able to state and apply the first law of thermodynamics*). (*Note to facilitator:* You can either bring examples or have the participants generate them.)

In small groups, have participants choose three or four of the sample objectives and design two or three assignment options for each, using a variety of learning styles. Also include a discussion about how to check for accountability with the students. (How will they demonstrate that learning occurred?)

Putting It Into Practice

(Extended activity)

Design similar options for your teaching objectives this week and implement them. Be prepared to return to the group to report on how things went and get feedback for modifications.

Chapter 13 Obstacle: I Have Neither the Time nor the Funding for All That

Chapter Summary

A common complaint heard from high school teachers regarding differentiation is a lack of time for planning and funds for implementing. This chapter gives teachers some strategies for both issues. Buddying up with colleagues for planning, making generic grading rubrics that work with multiple units, using student-generated ideas, and adding pieces slowly are all strategies to help with time constraints.

Most teachers have limited funds available for non-textbook teaching materials. This chapter encourages looking for nontraditional, common, everyday items to use, asking parents for old materials and books, checking with the district surplus folks, and making good use of your school media specialist.

Discussion Questions

1. Are there teachers in your department who may be willing to cooperate with you in the design of a teaching unit?
2. What do you currently have in your classroom—other than your adopted text—that can be used as teaching aids?

Activity

● *Thinking Outside the Box:*
 Find New Uses for Standard Materials

Time: 45–60 minutes
Materials: Old record albums (available from thrift stores for about a dollar), a package of sewing needles, a spool of thread, plain copy paper, a plain wooden pencil, and an assortment of "junk" such as paper clips, rubber bands, toothpicks, facial tissues, screws, and/or twist ties.

Divide participants into groups of three. Give each group one needle, a 2-foot length of thread, one piece of paper, a wooden pencil, *and* one of each of the other pieces of "junk" you've brought (don't mention which are the essential items and which are the junk—just dole out all the materials). Now let each group select one record album.

The assignment: "Using nothing more than the materials I gave you and your hands, you have 45 minutes to make your record play loud enough that I can hear it across the room. Begin!"

After 45 minutes, have a performance!

(*Author's note:* Yes, it can be done, and no, I will not tell you how, as there is no one right answer. You will be amazed at the creativity you find. If your group is full of fairly young people, you may at least have to tell them that records spin clockwise!)

Putting It Into Practice

(Extended activity)

Present some teaching objectives to your students this week and have them help you generate creative teaching assignment options for them.

Chapter 14 Obstacle: I've Been Teaching This Way for Years, and It Works

Chapter Summary

This chapter is one of the more important chapters in the book, in terms of showing how differentiation can benefit *all* classrooms. While teachers who have rather homogeneous groups of students may be finding success in traditional, lecture-based systems, even those students can benefit from adding some variety.

The two main areas of the brain involved in school learning are the hippocampus and the neocortex. The hippocampus is a quick, categorical memorization device. The neocortex is a much slower region that processes information and looks for relationships and patterns. We must involve the neocortex for long-term, practical working knowledge of a topic.

Emotion is a powerful glue to help cement learning events into place. Most people remember events with an emotional component for a long time—frequently for life. Try to make learning experiences novel so as to elicit emotion.

Hands-on learning is an excellent way to learn, as it targets the episodic as well as the semantic memory. Although they may be more time-consuming, elaborate, hands-on activities to culminate all the learning topics can activate the episodic memory system and then be cross-connected to the semantic system as well.

Teaching through the arts is probably the strongest avenue into an adolescent's brain. Due to the hormones associated with this age group, the hypothalamus area of the brain is particularly active. Arts directly target this region.

Discussion Questions

1. Share with the group a strong memory you have from your school days. After listening to others, do you agree or disagree with the idea that we tend to remember longest those events with emotional components?

2. Discuss the difference between "Statue of Liberty" classes (as described on page 104 of the textbook) in your building and higher-level elective classes. Do you see teaching strategy differences between them?

3. How can your school or department take better advantage of an adolescent's love for art?

Activity

● *The Power of Episodic Memory*

Time: 20–30 minutes
Materials: Overhead 3: The Power of Episodic Memory and the textbook *Differentiating the High School Classroom: Solution Strategies for 18 Common Obstacles*

Put Overhead 3: The Power of Episodic Memory (see back of this guide) on the overhead (or write them on chart paper). Reveal them **one at a time** and ask teachers to raise their hands (but not make a comment at this time) if they have a strong recollection of the date. Most likely, everyone will raise his or her hand at the last one. You can now go back and let them know the "events" that occurred on the other dates* and ask for recollections of things like:

- Who they were with on that day
- What the weather was like
- What they were wearing
- The color of the furniture nearby
- Any other recollection

Can you add emotional episodic events to culminating activities in the classroom to help students cross-connect memories as well? Discuss.

Putting It Into Practice

(Extended activity)

Try adding an emotional episodic event to a lesson this week. Report back.

Note to facilitator: Dates on overhead refer to:
June 5, 1968—Robert Kennedy assassinated
July 21, 1969—Man walks on moon
April 19, 1995—Oklahoma City bombing
August 31, 1997—Princess Diana's death
September 11, 2001—World Trade Center and Pentagon attacks

Chapter 15 Obstacle: There's No Support for It at My School

Chapter Summary

This chapter begins by acknowledging how difficult it can be to try something like differentiated instruction without any emotional support. Oftentimes this lack of support (or even opposition to your ideas) is the result of mental models of a differentiated classroom that involve chaos or watered-down curriculum. So sometimes administrative or department support can be increased by just educating school leaders on what a differentiated high school classroom looks like.

It is important for teachers to have some type of colleague or team support before starting instructional changes that go against the status quo of the school. A team can help with planning, implementation, and follow-up modifications.

Discussion Questions

1. Whom do you know within your department or school who may be interested in teaming with you on differentiated instruction?
2. How does your administration feel about a differentiated classroom? Do you need support in presenting your ideas to your administration?

Putting It Into Practice

(Extended activity)

● *Creating a Team for Differentiation*

Time: Ongoing event
Materials: Individual journals, planning materials, and the textbook *Differentiating the High School Classroom: Solution Strategies for 18 Common Obstacles*

After reading over the requirements for an effective team on pages 113–114, set up a working team or teams among your participants. Make a plan for design, implementation, and follow-up.

Chapter 16 Obstacle: My District Requires Me to Follow a Prescribed Text

Chapter Summary

Textbooks have been the hub of classrooms and curriculum for years and years. Parents view textbook availability as one of the strongest measures of school success. Unfortunately, most districts or schools have only one acceptable or allowable textbook, and therefore many teachers must use the prescribed one. Yet research shows that allowing students a choice in text is one of the most effective ways to increase both motivation and engagement in textbook reading.

In addition to increasing motivation and engagement, a variety of texts help ensure that students get multiple perspectives on a topic and help to catch inaccuracies that may exist in some textbooks.

If teachers are using textbooks for independent reading, they should use books that are at a readability level one or two grade levels below the grade they teach.

If teachers cannot vary the textbooks they use, they should look to supplement them with other texts, newspapers, newsmagazines, and trade publications in order to offer variety and keep information current.

Discussion Questions

1. Does your school give you more than one option for the textbook? If so, how can you obtain copies of each so that students can choose between texts?
2. What supplemental reading materials should you be stocking in the classroom to add variety and ensure that your information is current?
3. Do you currently share with your students how they are to use or be accountable for the information in their text? Reread Practical Solution Idea 16.2 on page 119, and discuss how the expected use of the information influences a student's reading strategy.

Activity

● *Determine the Readability of Your Textbook*

Time: 10–15 minutes
Materials: Each participant needs a copy of the textbook they use in their classroom, the Fry Readability Chart (easily found through

an Internet search), and the textbook *Differentiating the High School Classroom: Solution Strategies for 18 Common Obstacles*

The bottom half of the textbox on page 118 in the book explains how to determine the grade-level readability of your text using the Fry formula. Using sample passages from your text, determine its readability. Discuss whether this text is appropriate for how you use it in your classroom.

Putting It Into Practice

(Extended activity)

Add some supplemental reading materials to your classroom this week.

Chapter 17 Obstacle: Parents Expect Lecture Format in High School for College Prep

Chapter Summary

Many teachers feel justified using an exclusive lecture format in their classrooms, as they consider themselves teaching college prep courses, and they and their students' parents know how important lecture note-taking skills are for a college-bound student. For these students, a variety of note-taking strategies should be offered and taught.

But equally important is helping students understand what to do with those notes. Most of the learning and test preparation in college do not occur through note taking alone. Most of the learning comes with study and practice strategies. A differentiated classroom is an excellent strategy-teaching environment for those college-bound students.

This chapter includes research-proven strategies for increasing both motivation and engagement in textbook reading.

Discussion Questions

1. What strategies did you use in college to help you learn the material from your lecture notes? Can you share some of those strategies with your students?
2. Look at the examples of note-taking graphic organizers on page 125. Share with the group other organizers you have seen or used.

3. Discuss the strategies for increasing motivation and engagement found in the book on pages 125–127.

Activity

● *Increasing Textbook Engagement and Motivation*

Time: 20 minutes
Materials: Paper, pens, and the textbook *Differentiating the High School Classroom: Solution Strategies for 18 Common Obstacles*

Pair participants. Have them reread the Practical Solution Ideas 17.1–17.8 on pages 127 and 128. Through a sharing of ideas, have the teams discuss which of these might be workable in their own classrooms. Have them formulate and commit to a plan of action for the coming week.

Putting It Into Practice

(Extended activity)

Implement your plan (from above) and report back to the group.

Chapter 18 Obstacle: The Bottom Line—If They Are Learning, You Are Teaching

Chapter Summary

This chapter elaborates on the three sets to school learning—input, internalizing, and output—also known as teaching, studying, and testing.

Students who are nontraditional learners struggle with the input and output despite being very good at internalizing the learning. Given that the purpose of school is to learn, we should not let the limiting ways we traditionally have presented input and output segregate and dismiss these nontraditional learners.

Discussion Questions

1. Discuss the author's statement on page 132, "What is disabled is an education system that cannot effectively teach to a young mind that is perfectly capable of learning." Do you have personal experience with this statement?

2. Discuss in the group the key ideas from this book as they are summarized in this final chapter.

Activity

● *Concluding Poster Session*

Time: 45+ minutes

Materials: Chart paper, markers, and the textbook *Differentiating the High School Classroom: Solution Strategies for 18 Common Obstacles*

Read aloud to the group the last section on page 132, "Practice Assignments for Overcoming This Obstacle: Be Part of the Solution." Allow a moment for self-reflective thought.

With a partner, create a poster titled "Why Teach?"

Share it as the poster session description earlier in this guide, under Activities in Chapter 5.

Journal Prompt

What have you gleaned from this book and this study group that has changed your view of teaching? What behavioral changes have you seen in yourself? What plans for change are in your future?

Overheads and Activity Sheets

Overhead 1: Workshop Starter

This book is dedicated to the wildlife of the Allegheny Mountains—the dragonflies, pileated woodpeckers, turtles, wild turkeys, screaming eagles, the cacophony of frog voices, salamanders, black bears, raccoons, and deer. They all provided inspiration during the writing of this book by allowing me the experience of a different kind of diversity. In the wilderness or in the classroom, every creature brings unique gifts from above. Beauty is to be found in the blending of those gifts. Celebrate the symphony.

Overhead 2: Differentiated Instruction

This is *NOT* differentiated instruction:

For my unit on eukaryotic cells we'll use:

- FLASH CARDS for learning vocabulary
- WORKSHEETS for reinforcing the TEXT
- SMALL-GROUP project for learning the plant/ animal cell differences
- LECTURE for learning the organelle functions
- LARGE-GROUP DISCUSSION for review

This *IS* a better plan for differentiated instruction:

For my unit on eukayotic cells, we'll use:

- FLASH CARDS or SMALL-GROUP project for learning vocabulary
- LECTURE for reinforcing the TEXT
- SMALL-GROUP project or WORKSHEET for learning the plant/animal cell differences
- TEXT or LECTURE or VIDEO for learning the organelle functions
- LARGE-GROUP DISCUSSION for review

Overhead 3: The Power of Episodic Memory

June 5, 1968

July 21, 1969

April 19, 1995

August 31, 1997

September 11, 2001

Activity Sheet 1: Differentiating All Three Learning Areas

Choose a unit topic from your current content area. With a colleague, generate some ideas for differentiating each of these three areas.

Unit Topic: _____

Ideas for differentiating the CONTENT:

Ideas for differentiating the PROCESS:

Ideas for differentiating the PRODUCT:

Activity Sheet 2: Layered Curriculum®

Unit Topic: _____

Start Date: _____ **Finish Date:** _____

C Layer Objective(s)	Assignment	Points
(Day 1 or) Objective 1:	1. 2. 3. 4.	
Objective 2:	1. 2. 3. 4.	
Objective 3:	1. 2. 3. 4.	
Objective 4:	1. 2. 3. 4.	
Objective 5:	1. 2. 3. 4.	

(Continued)

Activity Sheet 2 (Continued)

B Layer Objective(s)	Assignment	Points
	1.	
	2.	
	3.	

A Layer Objective(s)	(Essential Question, Current Event, Debatable Real-World Topic)	Points
	1.	
	2.	
	3.	

Materials to Gather	Things to Copy

Assessments:

Workshop Evaluation Form

Content

- How well did the seminar meet the goals and objectives?

- What professional support will you need to implement what you have learned from this seminar?

- How well did the topics explored in this seminar meet a specific need in your school or district?

- How relevant was this topic to your professional life?

Process

- How well did the instructional techniques and activities facilitate your understanding of the topic?

- How can you incorporate the activities learned today into your daily professional life?

- Were a variety of learning experiences included in the seminar?

- Was any particular activity memorable? What made it stand out?

Context

- Were the facilities conducive to learning?

- Were the accommodations adequate for the activities involved?

Overall

- Overall, how successful would you consider this seminar? Please include a brief comment or explanation.

- What was the most valuable thing you gained from this seminar experience?

Additional Comments

SOURCE: Adapted from *Evaluating Professional Development* by Thomas R. Guskey, Corwin Press, 2000.

Notes

CORWIN
PRESS